AF335599

WALKING at BRIGHTON

Dave Margoshes

▲ ▲ ▲

WALKING at BRIGHTON

THISTLEDOWN PRESS

Canadian Cataloguing in Publication Data

Margoshes, Dave, 1941-

  Walking at Brighton

  Poems.
  ISBN 0-920633-54-4 (bound) -- 0-920633-55-2 (pbk.)

I. Title.

PS8576.A74W3 1988   C811'.54   C88-098117-2
PR9199.3.M36W3 1988

Book design by A.M. Forrie
Cover painting by Douglas Thiell

Printed and bound in Canada by
Hignell Printing Ltd., Winnipeg

Thistledown Press Ltd.
668 East Place
Saskatoon, Saskatchewan
S7J 2Z5

Acknowledgements

Many of these poems have appeared in one form or another in: *Alchemist, Ariel, Bite, Canadian Author and Bookman, Canadian Literature, Chelsea Journal, CVII, Fiddlehead, Freelance, Grain, Hey Lady, New York Quarterly, Poetry Canada Review, Queen's Quarterly, Shaded Room, University of Windsor Review, Waves* and in the anthology *New Voices* (Mosaic Press, 1984). Some of these poems were broadcast on CBC's "Alberta Anthology."

The author would like to thank Paddy O'Rourke and Glen Sorestad for their sharp-eyed editing of this book.

This book has been published with the assistance of the Canada Council and the Saskatchewan Arts Board.

For ILYA, of course
and for Esther
and with thanks to Paul Cubeta, who taught me how a poem
means

CONTENTS

9 Season of Lilac
10 To the Source
11 Bouquets of Days
12 Thin Ice
14 Pas de Deux
15 Twenty Questions

16 Walking at Brighton
18 Where My Father Sat
19 The Barber's Chair
20 White Fruit
22 New Math

23 Weather Report
24 Length of Reach
25 Winter in Tehran
26 Coal and Straw
27 Halley's Comet
28 Good Medicine
29 Manana Comes at Last

30 Woodsman, Woodsman
31 Beneath the Skin
32 Arithmetic
33 As If
34 White Teeth
35 Calling the Moon to Dance
36 Namesake

37 Marking Time
38 This Is the Eleventh Time
40 IOU
41 The Way Ahead
42 Remembrance Day
44 Times Ten
45 Winter Passed

46 Bouquet
48 Alberta Fern
49 Saigon Rising
50 To Seize the Day
51 Disconsolate Dogs
52 Feel No Pain
54 Sartre Died for Our Sins

55 Beneath the Seawall
56 In Turn
57 Wait for the Ocean
58 On the Way Back from Peekskill
59 World Series
60 This Time the Wind
61 High Country
62 Landed
63 On Being 40

Season of Lilac

In april you come to me again in lilac
fall on my cheek like rain
take my hair like wind.

it is the *sense* of you the heat
brings in august, when life glistens
on skin and earth's deep smell climbs
high, bursting the veins of leaves
with the kind of joy birds know
as night cocoons to day, seasons turning

and december falls with the clear breath of you
sweetened ice on my tongue;

fall is the time when days drift
to sea to smother sand with damp wings
and your eyes touch fire, causing spark.

the seasons are full with you
the calendar rattles its leaves
for a glimpse of time's reflection
racing through my blood—
leaves fall, grass strains for wind
the soggy sky shakes itself dry
like a dog in from the snow to the fire
and love climbs like smoke
seeking its own level.

in april, then, you come to me in lilac
fall on my cheek like warm rain
take my hair like gentle wind
call me to lie down in fragrance.

To the Source

Walking today, we came to the empty creek bed
filled with promise and clots of snow,
rocks lifting hard faces to the sun
like debutantes waiting to be kissed
but no water where there should be
among the bones of summer.
This absence is a reproach,
an empty pocket,
a hole in the sky god peers through.

We follow the bed up, across a dry field
into trees thick as traffic,
listening for distant applause
water moving across stone.
"Listen," you say
and up we go, breath rattling,
leaping through islands of rotting snow,
faces stinging from branches
to the source.

Sunlight filters through branches
to brighten your eyes when you see it,
electricity running naked, hissing,
and you sing to the creek
follow it down till it disappears in snow
back to the heart of earth.
"Where does it go?" you want to know
and heading back, through a field jangling
with yellow and violet we missed before,
you sing to the flowers, to sun and sky,
sing to the water, sing of the source.

The earth stretches, shakes itself
like the dog in from the lake,
giving off heat and light—
love rises from its coat,
into your eyes.

Bouquets of Days

your hand slices apple time
you spit out years
        onto a china plate
you peel a rind of trouble
        from the core of love

those seeds—you put them in the ground
where they grow days
blossom up as thunder
taking life from light
reach for sky as a bird breaks night

those days—we slice the stalks
arrange them in water
let them shine through the dark
let them lay their hand of fragrance
        on us like a mist
keeping us safe—
when they wither
        we stack them in a corner to dry

we keep bundles of days as keepsakes
bouquets of days as a promise

Thin Ice

The secret is in getting
   the water to go hard—
any damn fool can cut
   a sawtooth hole,
   drop a line through,
   pull out fish dying
    to bare whiteness of flesh to air;
anyone can put skates to it,
   spitting chips into the sun's tongue
   with froth like albino blood
   so pure you can't tell
    heart from brace of bone,
slide blades across the bare face of it
   like fingers through washed hair,
    giving warmth back.

That's not the problem.

And neither, with love,
   is washing your face with it the thing—
splashing it up till
   hair plasters down,
that's easy as it sounds;
flying isn't what's hard,
   neither getting up there
   or staying aloft while sun
    melts your hold
or landing on a branch
   thin as ladyfingers
    without ruffling leaves,
all that's so damned easy there's
   no need to talk of it.

And *giving* is no tough tree to climb
    though taking can give you a shake
if you're not ready for it,
and slipping into the long
    sweet slide past suppertime
      is just that: a sleepy slide,
        with sweet friction to hold it in place.

None of those are the problem.

The *secret* is in getting love to set,
like Jello after you've sliced in the banana—
getting it into the shape it's supposed to be,
coaxing the brittle edge to bare its teeth
to the squinting blue sky.

Pas de Deux

this time we hear the music and dance

we don't turn away like before,
we rise and fall, air on sun
giving back the things we took away

this music gets into you:
takes you where you've never been
pries between your bones
whispers through you like wind
leaves a stain of memory

between songs, I take your hand
    night falls
        sky turns
            rain bends down
                and earth shimmers
we stand and feel the pulse

if you should say the things we know
if I could hear the end of night
if we could dream the beginning again
    like a child waking
        wiping away the taste of death

the music begins,
    someone beckons,
        we dance

Twenty Questions

how do I love thee? let me count the ways:
rain and morning light,
evening and smoke,
heat rising from rivers,
puppies' breath and Blue's white ear,
San Francisco, the wharf at Monterey,
Chinatown, the falls behind the curve
of the hill where light takes the breath
away from earth's green secret;

first snow, lifting its breast
to be kissed by god's chill teeth,
strawberries and cream,
white chocolate before it made your ear ache,
ferryboats, jars of sweet grass
from the drying oven,
ice cream sodas at that place on Jeffrey
where the funny girl with Iowa cheeks
pronounced soft benedictions with the syrup;

green stones, turqoise
from Taos, Navajo pots
brittle as love's cool skin,
bed boards, Agatha Christie
and lilacs in profusion, lilacs
the color they should be, pale
as the closing of eyes, soft as butter,
in alley hedges tall as distant fathers,
lifting their scent of heaven like a message.

Walking at Brighton

for Esther

This afternoon on the beach
I was reminded of autumn walks at Brighton,
wind breaking at our backs,
cold sand in our shoes,
funny shells and jellies on the rocks that moved,
our father walking with a cane—
a *stick*, he called it, as if to give dignity
to a prop of his own imagination—
and a scarf around his head to keep from hearing the air,
our mother in shoes that squeaked on the slats,
holding us from harm by calling us back from the sea
like fish struggling on a line which fed us life,
connecting us to land we long to reach.

I was ashamed of that scarf, of course,
the sticks and the squeaking shoes with rubber soles
unimaginably thick, and now I feel shame
for *that* shame, regret for things I could have held,
but the sand was so cold, the wind so fierce,
the days so long then

I don't imagine you remember any of this—
you girls were so much older,
so much closer in height if not age to them
and I was a stranger in the family,
always walking behind where the view is different,
always looking up;
you were so much older and the air between us
could be colder than the sand, filled with shame
that now becomes regret, like other things
that slip between our fingers.

I am reminded today,
as I sit on sand that is warmer than age,
watching my wife and our dog dance in the waves
while a faint wind tugs at my hair,
that you are 40 today,
an age unimaginable as rubber soles were to me then:
what causes me wonder is not that you have lived this long,
two generations, a decade less than half a century,
but that so much time could have elapsed,
time in which the squeak of our mother's shoes
reverberates like a seabird's harsh caw,
time in which our father's head has never yielded
to the detemined flailing of the wind,
time in which my step behind you draws closer
and the air we share grows warm,
welding time to time.

Where My Father Sat

Where my father sat
the cushions bent
with the weight
of ages and blood
running in his bones
like torrents to drown
the towns
we children built,
crusting foundations
scarred with silt.
The springs groaned
when his texture breathed.

Where my mother sat
the air rose giddily
into the swell of her skirt,
the air was glad.

The Barber's Chair

Sitting in the barber's chair
today as the razor drones
in my ear like bees whispering
secrets from the Incas
I see my father's face emerge
from beneath my beard
sudden as a bird
bursting from tangled branches
into the sieving snow.

For the smallest moment
we stare at each other,
me alive and here,
swaths of grey hair
mixed with black
in pools on my lap,
he dead a decade
but there in the mirror
just the same,
the smallest, smuggest
of smiles entwined
around the corners
of his lips,
lips that wouldn't lie

but I open my mouth
with surprise and they do.

White Fruit

for Judy

We are the children
our parents warned us against,
breaking hearts of mothers
who can only be ourselves:
taking wrong sustenance,
neglecting posture and sleep,
not living as truly
as they might have liked.

Even the sense of family
our mother knew has crumbled,
bonds of trust like mushroom heads
crushed by buffeting winds:
you have yours, our sister hers,
I mine—as much distance and time
between us as the sticky web
separating stars:
we call and write on expected intervals,
make pilgrimages like stunned arabs
in bethlehem for nieces' sake,
giving them glimpses of communities
both larger and smaller than the ones
they could fashion on their own.

How unlike her own brothers and sisters
we are: our mother's people
scattered, as we did, then drew together
like fingers in a closing fist,
mushrooms pushing their brave heads
into the cold air prematurely,
taking close comfort
in their neighbours' gills,
umbrellas against the unexpected elements.

Still they made her cry when the time came,
weighing her down with silver chains,
fairy rings of celebration,
mouths filled with glittering teeth
biting through smiles, drawing blood,
and here I am now,
repeating the ritual
with reminders from a distance,
nothing learned from personal history.

The day hangs a pivot, a hinge
to time's own door, and as you pass through
memory spins a bright coin for me,
the way she cried out,
tears silvering her flushed cheeks,
not merely tears, but pain,
and my own confusion:
was it *they* she cried over, the way
they had deserted her with their closeness,
or herself, the line she had tried to draw,
the adage she had left for us?
And will we, in blind love,
make you cry, reminding you
of time slipping past, stars
winking out in the heartless sky?

Their love took the form
of pieces of silver, strung together
into constellations.
Our is white fruit, fragile as ancient paper
but filled with pungent juice—
stalks firm in love's vague mycelium,
spanning distance, time, generation,
drawing us together even in silence,
baring its teeth at the indifference of stars.

New Math

for Judy and Gerson

we were three, we children,
now we are six
we were five in the family,
now we are eight
with the children eleven

we were six for a while,
the family,
then seven
then six again,
then, with the children,
seven and eight,
then we were nine
and another child ten

now we are eight,
with the children eleven.

the sum of the parts
is greater, at last,
than the whole
and the limits on addition
are subtracted by physical law.

we were three,
now we are six—
the fraction of love
is the difference.

Weather Report

i don't believe i'll wait till spring
to call down the spell
we need to set things right again:
this is the season seed catalogs come
and hyacinths would be shedding light
in the kitchen if we'd remembered to buy bulbs.

winter lasts too long to stand on ceremony,
life too short to look away
and love is fragile as snowflakes:
each one, science teaches, is different,
each a perfect creation
brittle as procelain, splinters
thickening into ice under foot.

radio says a break is coming:
winter can't last forever
and cold itself gets numb, loses feeling;
God belched in Alaska last night
and they felt the thunder half-way around the world.

there's a warm front moving in from sea,
calling down the spirits asleep in the pass,
nudging loose a shard of spring
sharp as ice, warm as breath:
chinook sucks down heat like quicksand
and just as fast, giving light
to the corners—and i'll be
god-cold-damned if i'll stand for any more:

i don't believe there's any chance
of just *waiting* out the storm
when you can open the window by yourself
and reach out beyond the air to where i stand.

Length of Reach

This was the winter the chinook came and stayed
past reason, like an uncle you love but can't
get rid of, slipping its warm tongue along
our necks to get at the salt, insinuating its
way past disapproval of natural order.

You were out much of the time, looking
for something that wouldn't come
into focus behind trees, beneath the lids
of god's eyes, asking whales for comfort they
couldn't afford to give, couldn't refuse.

The length of your reach defined the longing
hidden beneath your heart's blind spot, pushing
you farther out than you'd like to go, onto
ice crackling beneath your step like leaves;
behind you, I stood with line, ready to throw.

Winter in Tehran

That was the winter
    cold broke the pipes' heart,
    turned the lake's pastel tongue to teeth,
    sent us flying, animals before fire's rush.

The skies, day after day, were clear cold blue,
god's eye frozen straight through to heaven,
and we skated till our ankles went to Iran for peace.

Iran. That was the winter the city they named you for
broke open like the lips of a wound
and Cambodia shuddered beneath its thin coat,
cold breath rattling along its bones.

The university closed its eyes, shaking its head,
    the phone calls were wrong numbers.

Our friends fought.

But that was the winter you rubbed yourself together
    like kindling, stared the ice down,
    blew love on my hands. That was the winter
    you never stopped reading the ads
gave yourself the sky in trade for land—
that was the winter you pried open the shell,
    peered inside, basked in the light,
took what was coming with favor and grace,
    gave back more than expected.

Coal and Straw

Winter came late, setting us up
with a boxer's precision,
feinting us punchdrunk with sun
then pouncing, cat on a bird,
immune to the fluttering of wings,
heartless, cutting through to bone,
cold as teeth, silent as dumb snow.

The car gave us trouble,
your job ended but you found a new one,
the pipes froze and we had to burn earth
to get at where the septic tank
shrugged, refusing more neglect,
a sulking child insisting
on recognition for its accomplishments;

it was something you could understand.
In the embers of coal we heaped on snow
veins of straw turned to filigreed webbing
designed to press heat into the ground's heart,
black spider's drool breathing whispers
of spring in earth's numb ear:

in the teeth of cold, warm wind's tongue;
in the mouth of darkness, embers
glowing like flinty spittle;
after all these years, love a hand,
opening, counting its fingers,
astonished at the number.

Halley's Comet

bone cold november, fog at christmas,
first sign of rhubarb in january
a guy at the office tells me, elated,
he could be reporting a child's first steps—
rhubarb shoots tender as lovers' mouths
spearing their way through never-frozen ground
frogmen slipping silently into foreign water,
ready to strike a first blow.

the seasons continue to confound us here,
ocean at our left hand, mountains at our right
providing the only continuity—above us,
the celebrated comet lumbers across the heavens,
an uninvited guest hurrying to keep appointments,
unseen but sensed, like whales surfing
on intimate waves, just beyond human reach.

certain absences fester, traffic
droning beneath us, comets humming above:
you are often distant, I am away much,
travelling in uncharted territory within
ourselves, out of touch,
you are gone days and I nights
leaving only thin strips of time
for the two of us, bright ribbons
wrapping the package of our love.

life unravels, gathers together, goes on,
turns back on itself like the seasonal
passage of whales, the flight of comets
cast on through indifferent night regardless
of distance, atmosphere, attention spans:
each cycle, 76 years, a lifetime, a breath,
billiant snowball hurtling itself against light,
love burning fiercely, oblivious to pain.

Good Medicine

cold whistles down my back,
laughter not meant to be heard,
and fever slips its cat's tongue
across my blood's grain,
sandpaper bringing
eyes' sheen to night

i shiver and my dry mouth
closes on a taste of sickness itself,
a round opening in the sky
giving up to flights of air
where shadows pass over clouds
and rain falls without sound,
without light.

in the very centre of the heat
you trace a wand of lace,
a cool finger along my ribs,
you fill up the hole where sand
rushes through wounds,
you bandage my throat with your hair

i take you like medicine
you restore me
give me balance
give my shadow shape—
you make me well,
give me back the light.

Manana Comes at Last

Manana comes at last,
    sweeping away props holding time in check,
horizons always slipping beyond touch
    slam down and stand
    ready to be mounted—
the time we thought would never come
    engulfs us, seeps into our blood.

Here we stand then,
    the things we said we'd never do behind us,
bones of dreams in place,
    footprints filling in
    where we always feared to walk,
armour left to rust, forgotten,
    teeth of promises clamped shut.

You are the one who pulls me
    straight through to day's end,
your hand a beacon
    sluicing a path through time
    for me to walk,
I am the one who sends you letters
    reminding you of where we've been,
giving a glimpse of tomorrow.

Woodsman, Woodsman

for Pat and Mark

when the axe handle broke
he stopped everything to make a new one,
stripping an aspen stick down
to white meat clean as chicken's breast,
burning the ragged shaft out of the axe head
in a kindling fire we made on the beach,
wedging and nailing and binding it fast
till it was good as new—
better than new, he said,
looking at me like god inventing man,
then going back for woman,
"because it won't break,
this one'll bend."

then he went back to the woodpile.

all winter long, he'll sharpen down
the sky, use it to cut sawhorses,
the shed, the cabin, the cradle,
while I warm myself by his burning heart.

Beneath the Skin

for Jon and Bernadette

Secret lives beneath the skin
give shelter, sustain us,
keep promises lips never can,
whisper strength beyond hearing.

Joining hands is the visible part,
the dance performed—
what *isn't* said, the vow not taken,
lasts longest, peers back from the glass

sees what lies hidden
beneath the skin, camouflaged,
reminds us what begins doesn't end,
what ends fails to begin again

and the heart can splinter—
take care of love when it pierces
the skin, slivers of love
beneath the skin.

Arithmetic

for Pat P.

it's arithmetic, really
and simple stuff at that
—one from two equals one—
none of this new math stuff
nothing you'd need a calculator for
just the fingers of your left hand
where the ring used to be and now
color is returning to the skin
like snow sifting in on deer tracks
or light filtering back after a shadow.

the important thing to remember
is the difference in the columns:
loss is here, on the left
gain on the right, like dark and light
the trick is all in the balance
being on a high wire
with *down* all around you, peering up—
what you need to know
isn't the weight of the loss
or the color left behind
when you peel away the one
but the feel of the gain
smooth and hard like small round stones
in the palm of your hand
and the quality of light
shining from the other.

As If

for Peter Waylon Johnson

we went skiing last year
all of us bundled into your father's
new car and got lost on the
highway, listening to the radio
missed a turn, wound up
in milwaukee, spent the night

drank beer in the city
which made it famous
and slept deep, in drifts.

on the slopes the next day
your father distinguished himself
by falling fewer times than my
wife while your mother and i
kept their glasses warm by
the fire, toasted the sky

beneath which we were small
and took heat from the cold
they brought to us coming in.

in the night driving home
we stopped on the river, lost again
in the quiet air and listened
to the fish finding their way
beneath the drifts of stream
which never strays

over the trembling boards
of the bridge your father
drove, not looking back.

White Teeth

for Claire Harris

I didn't know you were brown,
didn't know your heart was clear,
didn't know your voice had rivers in it,
didn't know you eyes were trees

i didn't know your poems were white,
like teeth

Calling the Moon to Dance

for Pat and Allan

on the celebration of a moment which marks neither a beginning nor an end

the great shaggy beast comes in to the fire
like sudden breath, shakes off night's dust,
turns to stare down grass,
settles its menacing parts like embers
ingratiating themselves into snow's favour,
lifts its head one last time to wink away
darkness, lies motionless as heaven
settling down to do god's will.

breathless, we hide in its shadows
glowing like conspirators' teeth,
baring our own into love's sharp sparks,
sighing breaths deep as grass in August,
clinging to each other like strands
of silk coiled into musical hair:
our hearts sing to each other,
cicadas calling the moon to dance.

here, in the hollow of god's throat,
we make our refuge, two pauses in
a span of time that doesn't cease—
out *there* the world spins dumbly on
oblivious to the pain, senseless to joy;
we turn our backs to it as easily,
turn to each other, whisper a word:
blinded by light, we rage at darkness.

Namesake

for Susan Tanaka and Eric

like a photograph of the flowers
you gave me
i'll keep your name
pressed between pages
of my life
where i can find it
when the need comes

but you won't mind
will you
if on my wrist i wear my own
to remind you of the me
you love,
to keep myself in mind

and you say my name the way
the owl says to night:
come down upon me, cover me,
fold me in your light

Marking Time

marking papers, marking time
something skitters along the glass
to bring my eyes up, like wings,
mouths, splinters of sun/
ice baring its flesh to river's teeth/
dumbfounded robins, wings aching like hearts,
pecking at hollow bones of their fathers/
rain hissing through yellow breath of grass
rising from earth like raw bread—
two and a quarter million spiders per acre
Mark Trail says, grimacing, wrinkling their noses
open pockets, kissing secrets away
keeping us safe from lower forms—
spring unfolding as it should/
sky resigning itself to days deep enough to hurt,
like smiles that go on too long

this was the perfect time for us
to put our stamp on the way
time unwraps itself from the candy stick:
not quite a may pole but deep enough
into the season for a tension
sly as a tongue working a sore tooth,
like an angler working the first trout

this was the perfect day for us
to plant ourselves into the season
like a moon's change, weather turning/
leaves giggling out of grey hiding
into green laughter, love coming around:
everything coming to an end, sighing/
everything beginning again, like rain/
the heart marking time— but just for a moment,
catching its breath to begin again

This Is the Eleventh Time

This is the eleventh time
I've made the effort to gather up,
analyze, celebrate, heal
the fragments of space between us
and we might wonder at the purpose—
this compulsion on my part,
expectation on yours,
this *habit* of ours—
of compressing light into lines,
days into words,
meaning into flesh
to bind these naked, scarring bones.

I can't make myself believe
that's all there is to it,
that habit, more than all else,
takes the place of reason twice a year,
as in ritual, as if these words
were holy knives, purified
to sever the sores from flesh
sanctified in different ways.

I trust too much in other things
to take even myself at my word,
to believe in signs which appear,
opaque clues in a crossword,
to have no logical correspondent.
I know, from turning pages
till my thumbs flake into the grain
of pages still to be written,
from long moments of trembling
on the brink of some forgotten mystery
which cries to be known
like a worm beneath a falling heel, shouting out:
"Don't crush me, don't crush me,
I shall be beautiful and fly,"
and then the sublime fall, the moment of flight—
from all these things and more I know
there *will* be something to fit.

Is it habit, then,
to tell you I love you?
Yes and no, no more nor less
than breathing, sighing,
wanting to cry and failing—
compulsion to love you?
expectation to be loved?
a habit to do it and say it
and make it so much a part of life
that life without it is no more
than a photograph before
the shutter opens?

Words don't lie but their meanings do
and perhaps the fault we find
lies there, beneath the sound,
in the fleshy pulp, the quick of language;
if habit is the hand leading us to morning,
the touch opening our eyes,
the taste of night's madness,
the smell of light fragmenting,
the sound of petals bursting
this spring above the crack of clubs
pounding them down unmercifully,
then spare me the cure.

But caution: giving yourself up
may be hazardous
but giving up is not the way to begin.
One fold opens on another
and still another lurks beneath
the teeth of time, smiling, always smiling.
And who would have thought
it would last even this long,
who would have dreamed it would begin again?

IOU

This is for all the debts
real and imagined
built up over years,
interest
going both ways:

slights, offences
sleights of hand, impatience
abuses of grace
failures to deliver.
This is an IOU

not just for the river
but the banks beyond,
that girdle of land
tying water to earth,
keeping promises.

This is the caveat
you insisted of me,
all that I demanded of you,
all the encumbrance
our own law requires;

a debt to be paid off
one moment at a time
long as we want
at our own rate,
on demand.

This is for all the debts
we owe each other,
for the love you give me
without my asking,
for all the promises kept.

The Way Ahead

down this road snow's deep
and the bend never does end,
you want to ride it
you take your chances with the rest

but I been down here before,
it ain't so bad as some say:
mornings keep coming up
dark keeps slidin down
and the rain falls the same way here
as ever —hard and at a slant that cuts

there ain't no turnin back
and that's for the best most likely:
go round to places you been before
you find they're changed, so're you
and the ground is beaten down beneath your feet
like the grass bed of a dog
that ain't goin nowhere at all
and don't even have the sense to know why

that ain't the way to go
not for the likes of us
not when we know better
when we want more
when we goddamn well have to or die

the only thing to pay mind to
short of keepin on itself
is makin sure the way ahead is clear

I'll go first
now, quick, you follow

Remembrance Day

Somehow we let it slip by,
    that moment in time when
        in a different context
    nations bow their heads to pray,
that brave commemoration of
    the finest hour, the sweet
        horrible moment of testing.

But time clouds memory, even those
    of piercing sweetness, a head
        filled with toothpaste pain
    the clatter of inspiration
        whispers of promise
and it's so damned easy
    to drown out a whisper—
there it goes, a chip of time
    bobbing by on the river below,
        a stick of wood in high water
    invisible even from the bluff.

We sensed its coming, that moment,
    talked of it, unbelieving
        then let it slip by,
    the shadow of a bird when you
let your eyes fall, dazed by light,
    half a lifetime shudders by
        with no more sound than that

except it doesn't, really
    there never was one heart-stopping
      moment of sweetness, no awakening
    no time when the earth stood still
      only a beginning, a stripping away
of old skin to let nerves get at air:
    an opening, a new sense of contentment
in the lungs a smoker would understand
    new paths for blood to travel
from heart to fingers to heart again,
    and it isn't a moment we stop
      to remember but those that follow
    the winding of a clock with hands entwined,
      not a moment but a lifetime.

Times Ten

a wire running the century rim of time
    my love roams the circumference
        of our lives
encircling us, taking us within
    defining the borders that cross
        the naked surface without limit
threads of spider lace
    a flower breathes

here in the thin air above time
    at the farthest reaches of dream
        I cling to you
there is no border of dream
    no frontier protected enough
        to hold back the rush
to feel, to touch, to know
        that you and I are all

Winter Passed

Winter passed early this year—
  today I heard daylight scratching
   at the blind to make its break
    and sun ranged high across the eggshell
     skin stretched on filling trees
      like laundry out to dry
       one drop at a time

In your eyes I see summer flicker
  like coals raked up by wind
   giving light to the stone
    and your skin grows clearer now
     as days grow longer,
      pulling the haywaygon earth behind
       them, rosebuds in a cart

The time we spent *talking* about time
  evaporates in spring, cold comfort
   sizing up the day caught in the sun,
    too late to run for shelter
     and the weight of trying
      always trying
       lifts like heat fleeing earth

If I come to you now like fog,
  spelling the sun, closing in,
   breaking the chance for breath
    you know the refuge lies within me,
     deep in the greyest heart of time
      where all love springs, washing
       winter past

Bouquet

Died. Daisy and Violet Hilton, 60, Siamese twins who became a standard attraction on the old vaudeville circuit for three decades; of pneumonia; in Charlotte, N.C.

—news item, January 1969

Daisy, those things you said
about mother weren't true
I know—you had
no more sense of what
it was than I could have,
after all, could you?
But I forgive you now
even after all the pain
you caused; I know
that wound was yours
to share.

Violet, take hold
of me now like never
before; these shivers
which span this spin
we share is more
than love can bear.
In your hand I find
the touch I never felt
alone before,
the touch you said
we'd find.

Daisy, that dress we bought
in Dayton and wore
through San Diego
and all the rest
that final trip when we made that
awful film—
it was you it became the most.

Violet, there's just one thing
I never said,
one thing you never felt
when my blood took the news
across the span,
one secret I'll keep
for myself even now;
but hold me close
and I'll whisper.

Alberta Fern

died Feb. 16, 1977

This air we breathe
doubles back on us,
closes up a fist in the lung
pounding your back to dislodge
longing thick as bites of steak,
shutting down the sucking weeds
the way frogs' shadows
turn water lilies blood dark
under skies clear
as babies' milky breath.

It all goes around, doesn't it?
Van wheels slipping in deep snow,
turning nowhere the way
you turned to me,
the way you said things had turned—
back from Hawaii, you were ruddy-faced
like someone embarrassed by a glimpse
of herself through waves,
bathing bottoms torn away,
hair flowing like seaweed;
but after Mexico
you were pale as the underside of day,
white as the round of eye,
thin as falling lashes—
and there never really was a time
when the weather was right
to drive safely home.

Always there was snow behind the air,
something dark behind the light
waiting to scare the breath out of you.

Saigon Rising

April 29, 1975

i remember a man with blood on his hair
and a woman in a palace of fingernails
whose heart was chipped and bitten to the quick

that was the beginning of that country for us,
and *we* were just beginning:
i was riding in a bus through rain clouds
reading of men on fire
bombs falling like hail
to quench their thirst . . .
and you were going in circles,
your throat sore from drinking fire—
wherever we went
that country followed us
like true north or a fixed star
hanging cold over the dead sea—
there were times we thought the war would go on forever
but that we would perish in time,
that we would fall into slivers
while we held our ears against the boom of sighs,
there were times we thought there could be no end
to pain and loving was just a way of saving face

but today i see saigon rising
and the cobblestones soar into the light,
the crystal palace shatters:
today the blood dries in the air and the man
with white hair puts away his handkerchief
and today i hear the sigh end
like broken glass on the roadway being brushed away
by wind and the passing of time

that country is theirs, their time is now
and we too survived—
long after we thought it would have ended
the victory goes on

To Seize the Day

while mother made tea
we sat with our backs
to the wall drawing flowers
with our fingers in the frost

then the postman came
leaving footsteps like caves
all over the crusted lawn
and empty envelopes to play with

in our room
where we were sent
all was silent
all was still

and the light pressed hard
against the winded shutters
to break out
to seize the day

in the evening
there was soup
more tea and the teaspoon
and all the old stories again

Disconsolate Dogs

in memory, Stan Rogers

this is for Bruce Cockburn
    who lost religion
    found heat without light/
    noise, shiverless cold/
    the silence that comes
       between clouds when the power goes
    like god breathing out
       on starless nights

this is for Bob Dylan
    who found religion
    lost sense of being/
    sight, pain without scar/
    dying without the fear
       of knowing there's no going back
    like men without women/
       women without ribs

this is for Phil Ochs
    who read the headlines
    written on eyelids/
    heard the empty hand
    giving applause/
       smelled the rain without sense
    like disconsolate dogs
       left behind in the snow

Feel No Pain

A rare genetic disorder called dysautonomia affects the Ashkenazim, descendants of central and eastern European Jews: the few hundred children who are affected . . . feel pain but react to it with indifference. It is only through conscious effort that these children . . . avoid inflicting serious injuries on themselves. Even so, many do not survive into adulthood.
—newspaper medical column

Holocaust! Pogroms! A sea of blood
washing over generations, centuries,
fierce as Moses' uplifted eyes—
forget all that. It is as nothing.
Your words hurt me, but only
when I think to let it happen,
and nothing else, no more
history than the fire ring,
the sharp metal edge of my skates,
the rough concrete on my knees
when I fall, the sun's grim teeth
burning holes in other men's eyes.

I laugh in the face of dentists!
Tell bullies where to go for comfort,
neglect seat belts, try out for teams
whose demands exceed my bones' elasticity,
walk brazenly through glitter-night streets
where desire drips like spittle
flaunting gold chains, swaggering,
my smile filled with light, expectation.
Oh, world, come fill me up,
give me something I can remember.

Only my mother's rebuke
wounds me, the slight shifting
of my father's shoulders as he moves away,
the cast down eyes of that girl outside the *shul*.
Death itself is incomprehensible,
that smooth waking slide
into worlds without sight, sound,
the incessant counting.
I try hard, honestly, keep my eye
on the target as described,
stay alert, hands outside my pockets,
but nothingness holds no dread
when I have yet to be.

Sartre Died for Our Sins

Sartre died for our sins
   died to set us free
     took a turn along the boardwalk
     cast us like confetti to the sea
   laid us down across the sky
     died to let us be

Sartre died for our sins
   took the argument one step farther
     pushed his chin into the cloud
     jingling coins in his pocket
   put himself at the end of a line
     that has no other end

Sartre died for our sins
   we live on for his

Beneath the Seawall

Beneath the seawall
   where ocean, earth and sky
     melt down to crystal
time rushes under in waves
   pulled from the other end
     of our lives
making the crystal shine.

In a tidepool small as your hand
   I found a star, a piece
     of puzzle with jagged edges
and night's silent cry
   breaking to dawn—

overhead, great birds spin
   sparks from the wheel of god
     sharpening the day
flashing down to sea in sighs
   swelling upon wave and tide
     to turn again,
  pebbles flung to the sky
   skimming clouds
     that rarely come
sizzle into fog.

Here we live,
   stars caught in a tidepool,
     tied to sea and sky
pieces in a puzzle we hold
   the answers to
     in each other—

you come to me
   a bird of light,
     hover above me,
fluttering—
   I rise to you, a wave
     pressed from the flesh of sea.

In Turn

wild flowers turn down
and bare their necks to the wind
seek heat from the soil
where clouds cast no shadow

under this lid eyes fail to see
morning coming down
through black horizons
and grass blows up to scatter seed

this day comes,
waits, passes on,
goes by

little changes here
where season is a word
and one day after another
casts the sky in an endless role

the grass cuts a deeper shade
in spring, paler in winter
and wildflowers bend
to stem time

in a moment when time casts free
and love waits upon the water
for the tide to turn
and you to see

Wait for the Ocean

in this house, this spring
you come to me again
new as screens from sears,
their time finally delivered

your hair is white with it, this paint
your fingers black with earth
wrists scarred by rose thorns
your blouse sifted with flour

and i see you smile.

i too have blossomed in this atmosphere
cheeks ruddied and calloused palms
thumbs all sore from hammer slips
copper slivers embedded in my nails

and we wait for the ocean to warm
convinced that life will be better still
(as if it could)
and blow clean through these halls

forever the smell of paint.

On the Way Back from Peekskill

On the way back from Peekskill
we stopped for a minute
on the side of the road
for me to check the air.
To the east,
New York hovered over the river
like a strayed balloon,
heaving deep breaths
into its sooty lungs,
aching its jagged breasts.
The hollows dug out of the sky
by kites that afternoon
were still silting in
and soon it would be
as if nothing had ever happened.
The tires were OK
and our lights were clear—
behind the wheel,
the radio on,
you were asleep.

World Series

baseball is the game you never see, Tony,
like love standing sideways behind that poplar
or fish smiling up from mirror waves
at sky without sun,
the northern lights behind cloud.

yeah, but there are signs, Joe,
little things that make it the game
worth watching, like broken
yellow leaves where footsteps struck out,
leaving space for wind to fill,
love's shadow on early snow.

that's right, Tony,
and ain't that the way to go?

This Time the Wind

This time the wind gives shelter

breaks down from high land to low
like July rain, flowers
on its breath, pressing us against
earth's elbow where flatness runs on
forever, bends into the rise, a hawk
reeling on sun, leaving no mark

Beneath shreds of time cast down

snow bleeds into dust, giving itself
up as a dancer to point its sullen chin
upwind toward China across the pole, pulse
beating in its throat the way a bird's wings
defy heaven to make its stand again, try
the patience of gods

From the divide come all things that really matter:

water, wind, ice, fire—
time percolating to sand
breathing out a tired runner's sigh,
wind rattling time's crusted ribcage,
bearing down like morning
taking up the song

The earth really is flat, you know

mountains are illusions, rising smoke,
seas puddles of disappointed mariners' tears,
here in the wind's shelter only we are real—
these things we are, these names we put
to the things we touch, earth, fire, rain, ice:
the love we say beneath the wind

High Country

here are the mountains:
   beneath the high wind and tide
     of skies breaking under,
   beneath the last breath
     of spent stars
  we can climb
    taking stone for footing,
    sky for grip,
  darkness for the bind
    we didn't need.

rains turn to snow and back again
   and the sun takes refuge
     behind the earth,
      shivering,
      reappears like pride
   and the grass grows

the grass grows, melts
beneath sun's frown, dies,
the days fall like rain

here are the mountains:
   beneath the high wind and tide
     of skies breaking under,
   beneath the dark
    I come to you:

here is our love:
   high as the land
   deep as the sun

Landed

Driving west, chasing sun
   incessant day pulling us from night
      like a caterpillar, its time to fly come,
we edged off the road along the Colorado
   deep blue band of rubber tying the country together
its skin shimmering under pelts of sun
   like frogs' throats at dusk.
We lay in the steaming river in our clothes
   under some great stretching tree
      webbed with boys' ropes
   and felt at home:
water sifting through cloth and flesh
   to find its course in blood
blue compress of sky on our foreheads
   heat rising from our skin like flies,
we felt at home in a place we'd never been.

We stopped at a motel by a creek
rushing under our heads all night in song—
you said the water tasted like Beaujolais.

Landed now, 15 years later
   sailors washed ashore
snow melting under foot
   water tables turning
      rising like cold day breath
love's gravity holding us against each other
   something west pulling us forever
      out of night
light calling to darkness
   stars to rain
      land to bone
   water to blood
      seeking our own level.

On Being 40

Sun-drunk chickadee sputters toward the feeder
almost colliding with the window, bringing
a murmur from you, *oh god, he's inherited*
my clumsiness, the way the dogs do, then rights
itself like some liquid-boned ballerina
swings round to the green plastic cup, bobs head
lifts beak for a splinter of second to observe us,
throat pulsating, then quivers, darts, blends
into a flurry of light snow and sun lay down
to cover trails. Gone. Life simple as that.

Cold laying brittle teeth marks against skin/
stars distant as memory, hard as eyes turning away/
chinook winds sudden and warm as the baker's door
opening into dark Christmas streets/aurora borealis
lighting up sky like the entire corps
of the Royal Winnipeg sequined,
spinning out their fire, *the sky alive*, you cry,
pulsing with message like code
from the other side of heaven's opaque concave,
a pulse in the throat of god. Life complex as that,
that thick-tongued, after all—that far beyond reach.

Midway between dark and light, you can feel
the chill in the bird's bones, hear silence
pounding from stars' breath, surf on sand
in some far off california, sense the moment
coming and going with the flickering
irregularity of a bird at a feeder—midway
between god's left hand and right, you take
the time to set direction, choose rhythms/
holding your breath the better to hear
heart's distant clock murmur like wind.